# LISTENING STYLES PROFILE

## Facilitator's Guide

# Listening Styles Profile

## Facilitator's Guide

Kittie W. Watson, Ph.D
Larry L. Barker, Ph.D

Jossey-Bass
Pfeiffer
San Francisco

ISBN: 0-88390-466-7



Printed in the United States of America

Published by

Jossey-Bass Pfeiffer
350 Sansome Street, 5th Floor
San Francisco, California 94104-1342
(415) 433-1740; Fax (415) 433-0499
(800) 274-4434; Fax (800) 569-0443

Visit our website at: http://www.pfeiffer.com

Outside of the United States, Pfeiffer products can be purchased from the following Simon & Schuster International Offices:

Jossey-Bass/Pfeiffer
3255 Wyandotte Street East
Windsor, Ontario N8Y 1E9
**Canada**
888-866-5559; Fax 800-605-2665

Prentice Hall Professional
Locked Bag 507
Frenchs Forest PO NSW 2086
**Australia**
61 2 9454 2200; Fax 61 2 9453 0089

Prentice Hall/Pfeiffer
P.O. Box 1636
Randburg 2125
**South Africa**
27 11 781 0780; Fax 27 11 781 0781

Prentice Hall
Campus 400
Maylands Avenue
Hemel Hempstead
Hertfordshire HP2 7EZ
**United Kingdom**
44(0) 1442 881891; Fax 44(0) 1442 882074

Simon & Schuster (Asia) Pte Ltd
317 Alexandra Road
#04–01 IKEA Building
Singapore 159965
**Asia**
65 476 4688; Fax 65 378 0370

Printing 10 9 8 7 6

This book is printed on acid-free, recycled stock that meets or exceeds the minimum GPO and EPA requirements for recycled paper.

# CONTENTS

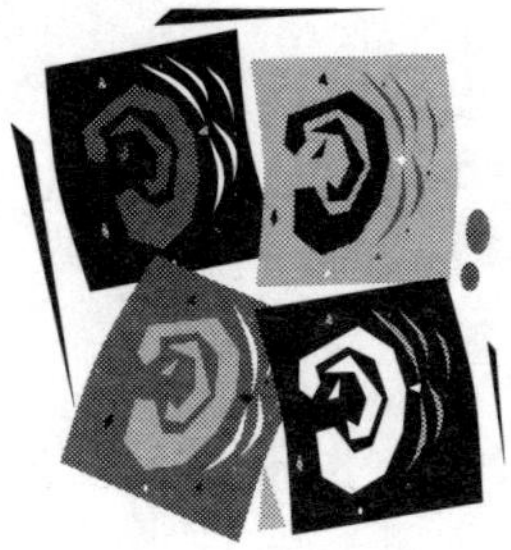

# Chapter 1
# UNDERSTANDING LISTENER PREFERENCES

People develop their listening habits from infancy. As a result, most people find it easier to listen to certain speakers and certain kinds of information than to others. For example, some people are more willing to listen to factual information or statistics, and others prefer to listen to personal examples and illustrations.

People also differ in their preferences of communication channels (telephone or face-to-face), message formats, structures, locations, and events. Rather than adapting their listening styles to different audiences and settings, most people habitually rely on their comfortable patterns of listening behaviors. These differences in the ways that people choose to listen are called *listener preferences.* Unknowingly, people make judgments and decisions based on their habits that may affect their communication effectiveness.

Because listener preferences are habitual responses that have been cognitively structured, practiced, and reinforced over time, these behaviors have become highly automatic. Recent research suggests that listening habits can be modified with incentive, knowledge, and practice (Dickson & Patterson, 1981; Smeltzer & Watson, 1984, 1985; Watson & Rhodes, 1980). Fortunately, it is possible to train people to adapt their listening styles to a variety of communication settings.

## Using the Listening Styles Profile

The *Listening Styles Profile* has been used and field-tested with thousands of participants in Interactive Listening seminars and programs throughout the United States. The instrument was designed to identify habitual listening responses and to encourage participants to think about how preference traits might be expressed in actual communication settings. By using the *Listening Styles Profile*, participants learn to adapt their preferred behaviors so that they match speakers' needs, time constraints, and listening settings.

## Benefits of the Listening Styles Profile

Most people do not think about changing the way that they listen, yet listening would be more efficient and enjoyable if they did. Everyone can benefit from using the *Listening Styles Profile*. One difficulty that people have is using only their preferred listening styles in every listening situation.

For example, a sales representative may become so involved in his sales pitch that he may finish the potential customer's sentences. By identifying his listening inclinations in certain settings, the sales representative can begin to make conscious decisions concerning whether or not to let a habitual preference dictate his actual listening behavior.

However, an executive may find it difficult, if not impossible, to switch her listening behavior. Because certain types of listening behaviors are reinforced at the office, the executive may have trouble changing those behaviors when she leaves the office. Instead of turning off her content-oriented listening behavior and using a more people-oriented one, for example, the executive continues evaluating and criticizing what her spouse, children, and friends have to say. It may be only when she is reminded to switch styles that she realizes that she is treating loved ones like employees.

## Features of the Listening Styles Profile

The instrument is easy to use and it can be scored and interpreted by participants themselves. Thus, participants quickly obtain a better understanding of the relationship between their listening preferences and those they avoid.

## PACT: Acronym Description

The acronym PACT outlines the four types of listening preferences presented in the *Listening Styles Profile:* **P***eople-oriented,* **C***ontent-oriented,* **A***ction-oriented,* and **T***ime-oriented.* Following is a brief overview of each preference that the facilitator should share with the participants after they have completed the instruments and filled out the grids:

*People Oriented.* People-oriented listeners demonstrate their preferences when they show care and concern for others' feelings, identify the emotional states of others, internalize/adopt the emotional states of others, or try to find areas of common interest with others.

*Content Oriented.* Content-oriented listeners demonstrate their preferences when they test or evaluate facts and evidence, welcome complex and challenging information, listen to facts before forming judgments and opinions, or favor listening to technical information.

*Action Oriented.* Action-oriented listeners demonstrate their preferences when they jump ahead and finish other people's thoughts, become frustrated by unorganized speakers, focus on inconsistencies and errors in messages, or show impatience when speakers ramble.

*Time Oriented.* Time-oriented listeners demonstrate their preferences when they set time constraints for their conversations and meetings.

## Listener-Preference Characteristics: Pros and Cons

Individuals with multiple listening preferences may switch back and forth among preferences in different situations and/or with different people. The following examples are designed to help participants think about how preference traits might be expressed in actual communication situations. Positive- and negative-preference characteristics are given after each example.

### People-Oriented Listeners

People-oriented listeners are most concerned with how listening influences their relationships with others. They listen to understand the emotional states of others and usually remain nonjudgmental.

When people are confronted with personal problems or crises, they seek out people-oriented listeners. Because these listeners are open to most types of people, they can become overly involved with others. In fact, at times, people-oriented listeners lose their objectivity when listening.

Consider the following example of how a person might demonstrate some characteristics of a people-oriented listener.

> Ted, a social worker within a large medical complex, scores high in people-oriented listening behaviors. His coworkers of fifteen years describe him as the most patient, caring, and open listener they know. Ted works hard at giving and receiving clear messages by asking questions, clarifying what has been said, and repeating what he has heard in order to clarify meaning.
>
> Unfortunately, Ted's listening preference is causing him trouble at work. Susan, Ted's supervisor, is concerned about Ted's ability to handle his caseload. For the last six months, Ted has failed to complete

his reports on time. Susan realizes that Ted spends too much time listening to his clients and that this overinvolvement with their problems has caused him to miss deadlines. Ted's listening behaviors illustrate some extreme characteristics of a people-oriented listener.

## Characteristics

The facilitator should have the participants read the following characteristics in the *Listener Profile Interpretation Guide* to learn more about people-oriented listeners' preferences. As the participants read the list, they should check the characteristics they notice most often in themselves or others.

**Positive Characteristics**

- ▲ Care and are concerned for others;
- ▲ Are nonjudgmental;
- ▲ Provide clear verbal and nonverbal feedback signals;
- ▲ Identify emotional states of others;
- ▲ Are interested in building relationships; and
- ▲ Notice others' moods quickly.

**Negative Characteristics**

- ▲ Are overinvolved with the feelings of others;
- ▲ Avoid seeing faults in others;
- ▲ Internalize/Adopt emotional states of others;
- ▲ Are intrusive with others;
- ▲ Are overly expressive when giving feedback; and
- ▲ Are nondiscriminating in building relationships.

## Action-Oriented Listeners

Action-oriented listeners concentrate intensely on the task at hand. They often prefer to listen to organized speakers and find it difficult to listen to rambling speakers. Action-oriented listeners are appreciated participants in most meetings because they encourage others to stay on the topic and to present information in a logical, organized way. However, because they appear to be overly task driven, action-oriented listeners may sometimes seem impatient and uninterested in building relationships with others.

The following example highlights several characteristics of an action-oriented listener.

Maria, an MBA student at a highly respected university, demonstrates traits of an action-oriented listener. As a working mother, taking classes at night, she is interested in getting the most information in the shortest amount of time. Although Maria avoided taking a required finance course from one professor with a reputed rambling teaching style, she finally had no choice and enrolled for the class.

Maria left the first class feeling frustrated and bored; she had not learned anything new. She was determined to make the next session more productive and went in prepared with a series of specific questions that helped the professor stay on track.

## Characteristics

The facilitator should have the participants read the following characteristics in the *Listener Profile Interpretation Guide* to learn more about action-oriented listeners' preferences. As the participants read the list, they should check the characteristics they notice most often in themselves or others.

### Positive Characteristics

- Get to the point quickly;
- Give clear feedback concerning expectations;
- Concentrate on understanding the task at hand;
- Help others focus on what is important;
- Encourage others to be organized and concise; and
- Identify inconsistencies in messages.

### Negative Characteristics

- Tend to be impatient with rambling speakers;
- Jump ahead and reach conclusions quickly;
- Jump ahead or finishes thoughts of speakers;
- Get distracted easily by unorganized speakers;
- Ask blunt questions;
- Appear overly critical; and
- Minimize relationship issues and concerns.

## Content-Oriented Listeners

Content-oriented listeners have a tendency to carefully evaluate everything they hear. At times it appears as if they are looking under a microscope and dissecting information. They prefer to listen to experts and highly credible sources. Content-oriented listeners can see all sides of an issue and enjoy listening to challenging or complex information. As bosses or managers, content-oriented listeners may hinder spontaneous discussions and the creative exchange of ideas.

Content-oriented listening behavior is often preferred by people with technical degrees or interests. Following is an example of a person with several content-oriented listening preferences.

> Carol is participating in her company's management program. She has a graduate degree in engineering and is admired for her excellent analytical skills.
>
> During Carol's first meeting of the day, a salesperson tries to sell her company a new product. As he begins his presentation, Carol evaluates his credentials and speaking style. She also makes mental and written notes about his presentation. Carol interrupts his presentation to ask a question about one of his services. At the end of the presentation, she summarizes what he said, expresses her reservations, points out what she considers to be the strengths of the product, and recommends that the salesperson prepare a proposal addressing her concerns.

## Characteristics

The facilitator should have the participants read the following characteristics in the *Listener Profile Interpretation Guide* to learn more about content-oriented listeners' preferences. As the participants read the list, they should check the characteristics they notice most often in themselves or others.

**Positive Characteristics**

- ▲ Value technical information;
- ▲ Test for clarity and understanding;
- ▲ Encourage others to provide support for their ideas;
- ▲ Welcome complex and challenging information; and
- ▲ Look at all sides of an issue.

**Negative Characteristics**

- ▲ Are overly detail oriented;
- ▲ May intimidate others by asking pointed questions;
- ▲ Minimize the value of nontechnical information;
- ▲ Discount information from nonexperts; and
- ▲ Take a long time to make decisions.

## Time-Oriented Listeners

Time-oriented listeners are conscientious about time and encourage others to be the same. They are direct in how they value time and often become impatient with others who waste it. Although time-oriented listeners encourage efficiency and time management, their self-imposed time constraints can limit creativity. They must be careful not to interrupt speakers and/or discount relationships with others.

Many time-oriented listener behaviors are easily identified in those who work in business and industry. Following is an example of a person with several time-oriented listening preferences.

> Bob is a partner in an international law firm. Many of his staff members often see him referring to his calendar or looking at one of his clocks when he talks with them.
>
> About midafternoon Bob's managing partner sticks his head in Bob's office and asks "Do you have a minute?" Bob responds, "Sure, I have ten minutes, but then I've got to finish that client-status report you wanted." Before starting the meeting, Bob closes his door, asks his secretary to hold all calls for the next ten minutes, moves what he has been working on to the side of his desk, and gives his partner his undivided attention.

Although Bob is conscious of time, he is also able to focus on important issues. The time-oriented listening traits that Bob uses in his business setting are usually valued. However, these same traits may be considered troublesome at home or with friends.

### Characteristics

The facilitators should have the participants read the following characteristics in the *Listener Profile Interpretation Guide* to learn more about time-oriented listeners' preferences. As the participants read the list, they should check the characteristics they notice most often in themselves or others.

**Positive Characteristics**

- ▲ Manage and save time;
- ▲ Set time guidelines for meetings and conversations;
- ▲ Let others know listening-time requirements;
- ▲ Discourage wordy speakers; and
- ▲ Give cues to others when time is being wasted.

**Negative Characteristics**

- ▲ Tend to be impatient with time wasters;

- ▲ Interrupt others;
- ▲ Let time affect their ability to concentrate;
- ▲ Rush speakers by frequently looking at watches/clocks; and
- ▲ Limit creativity in others by imposing time pressures.

## Multiple Preferences

It is not unusual for people to have high scores in two or more preference categories. In some cases the preferences complement each other, and in other cases they contradict each other. For example, if some of the participants have strong people-oriented and time-oriented preferences, they might be more open to conversations in some settings and appear rushed in others.

Following is an example of a person with multiple listening preferences.

> Alice, a bartender, alternates between being people oriented and time oriented. Of the four bartenders who work the evening shift, she has the largest number or regular customers. One reason for her popularity is the interest and involvement that she shows her customers, especially early in the evening when the lounge is not busy. At that time of night, she listens intently to her customers' stories, problems, and heartbreaks. Alice, like most people-oriented listeners, is often more interested in stories than in the details of taking orders.
>
> As the bar gets busier, Alice frequently begins to feel time pressure and her people-oriented preference is gradually replaced with her time-oriented preference. When she becomes time oriented, her willingness to listen to casual conversation decreases. Alice begins to ask her customers more direct questions concerning their orders and to demonstrate through her facial expressions that she is becoming impatient. She occasionally confuses her regular customers who are not used to seeing her when the lounge is busy.

When multiple listening preferences exist, there are several factors that can determine which preference will dominate or surface at a given time. Some of the primary factors include the following:

- ▲ Time pressure;
- ▲ Interest or motivation in speaker/topic;
- ▲ Communication setting;
- ▲ Presence of significant others during communication; and
- ▲ How much listening energy an individual has.

## Guidelines

Following are some guidelines for determining when one listening preference may predominate over others.

*People Oriented.* The people-oriented listener preference predominates when the following conditions exist:

- ▲ A relationship with the speaker is highly desirable.
- ▲ The setting for listening is informal or intimate.

*Action Oriented.* The action-oriented listener preference predominates when the following conditions exist:

- ▲ The listener has a low supply of energy to listen.
- ▲ The setting is more formal than informal.

*Content Oriented.* The content-oriented listener preference predominates when the following conditions exist:

- ▲ The listener is highly interested in the topic or speaker.
- ▲ The setting is professional, or the conversation is business related.

*Time Oriented.* The time-oriented listener preference predominates when the following conditions exist:

- ▲ Time pressure exists.
- ▲ The task is more important than the relationship with the listener.

## Listening Avoidance

Some participants may not be able to identify their listening preferences on the *Listening Styles Profile.* If they scored zero to three in all of the categories, they may tend to habitually avoid listening. Listening avoidance is not necessarily a negative trait, but it can cause problems if it is taken to an extreme. If the scores suggest that some participants avoid listening, those participants need to consider how this avoidance may affect their work and family relationships.

At times, listening avoidance may be a temporary state involving listener burnout. Executives and individuals in the counseling professions often experience listening overload. At other times it may indicate a person's preference to receive information from channels other than listening (for example, reading).

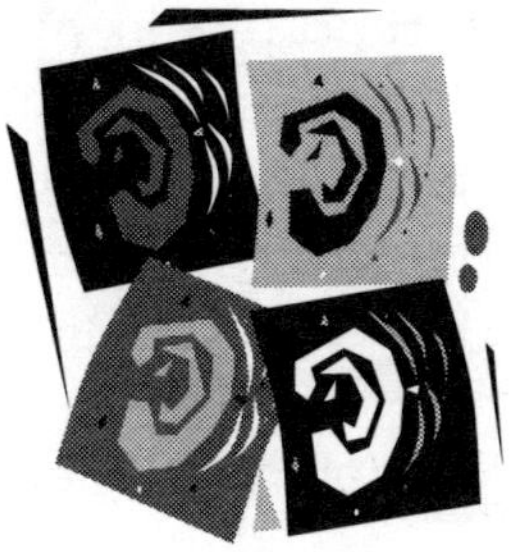

# Chapter 2
# INSTRUMENT DEVELOPMENT AND VALIDATION

As consultants to business and industry and professors in university settings, the authors noticed how people demonstrate different verbal and nonverbal behaviors. As the authors discussed the differences, they identified characteristics that seemed unique to certain professions, age groups, personality types, and genders. These discussions generated questions about how behavioral differences might affect listening comprehension and retention.

## Validation

Initial items for the *Listening Styles Profile* were generated from listening behaviors identified in a systematic review of the literature on listening as well as the authors' professional experiences. A pool of listening experts then screened the items. The first instruments included thirty items each and were administered to several pilot groups to test for contextual understanding and ease of administration (Watson, 1984). After item analysis, the instrument was refined to include twenty-four items that were later subjected to factor analysis (Mahon, 1991; Watson & Barker, 1988).

Preliminary test results identified four categories of listener behavior. Descriptive labels that reflected the differences among the listening behaviors were given to the categories. As the *Listening Styles Profile* has been refined, the descriptive labels have been modified to clarify category traits and to avoid a positive or negative word-association bias.

The factor analysis, as reported in Mahon (1991), validated the four categories that had been observed and described in earlier analyses. However, some of the twenty-four items in the instrument did not load heavily on a single factor. Two additional versions of the *Listening Styles Profile* were subjected to factor analysis following Mahon's (1991) study. The results of the additional factor analyses were used to revise items in the current version of the instrument (Watson, Barker, & Weaver, 1992; Weaver, Watson, & Barker, 1993).

## Gender Differences

Listening differences between the genders have generated considerable interest. The authors' data gleaned from testing with the *Listening Styles Profile*, support research that identifies gender differences in task listening versus relational listening (Boice, Hanley, Gansier, Shaughnessy, & Dudek, 1984; Booth-Butterfield, 1984).

The authors' results suggest that men and women listen with different purposes and goals: Females prefer the people-oriented listening style, which is aligned more closely with a relational rather than a task orientation. Conversely, the males prefer a content-oriented or action-oriented listening style, which is aligned more closely with a task rather than a relational orientation.

Results from instrument testing also support findings that suggest differences between men and women in conversational sensitivity (Berryman & Wilcox, 1980; Ray & Bostrom, 1990; Wheeless, 1984), interrupting behavior (Exposito, 1979; Kennedy & Camden, 1981; Smeltzer & Watson, 1986), empathy (Hanson & Mullis, 1985; Trotter, 1983), and situational contexts (Aries, 1987; Carli, 1989; Mabry 1985).

## Multiple Preferences

The *Listening Styles Profile* research results also suggest that multiple listener preferences are common among people. According to the results, 40 percent of the population in the United States has high scores in two or more listening-preference categories. When there are two or more preferences, the preference types are more likely to be people/content for females and action/content for males. There is currently no indication as to whether or not these listening preferences may complement or contradict one another. Even so, when an individual demonstrates more than one listener preference, his or her contradictory listening behaviors may be confusing to others.

## Listening Avoidance

The instrument research results also suggest that a significant number of people have no listener-orientation preferences. These individuals may tend to avoid listening situations, and the results would suggest that they may prefer to receive information through a communication channel other than hearing.

Significantly more men than women reported no particular listening preference. This result may be attributed in part to a phenomenon mentioned in listening-socialization literature, which suggests that boys and girls are reinforced for different manifesting communication skills (Booth-Butterfield, 1984; Seiler, Schuelke, & Lief-Brilhart, 1984).

Listening avoidance is not necessarily a negative trait, but it may cause problems if taken to an extreme. The total avoidance of listening—regardless of the situation, context, topic, or person involved—needs to be examined carefully.

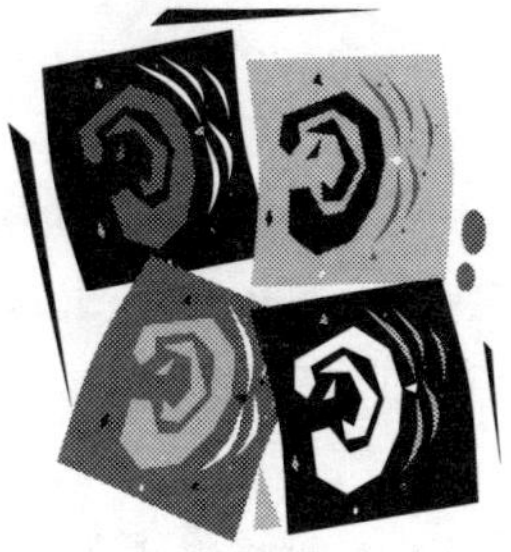

# Chapter 3

# UNDERSTANDING OTHERS' LISTENER PREFERENCES

In 1971 Nierenberg and Calero published *How to Read a Person Like a Book*. They suggested that people can determine what others are thinking and feeling by observing specific nonverbal cues. Some people are like open books and are easy to read. Others, however, are like books that have not been translated into our language.

People can determine an individual's listening preference by observing him or her carefully. The best listeners know how to "read" an individual's cues so that they can communicate with him or her most effectively. People need to learn to listen and adapt their messages to the preferences of each listener. Discovering listening habits, behaviors, and preferences is the first step toward self-awareness. Once the participants have uncovered information about themselves, they will need to learn about others' listening traits and preferences.

## Listening Styles Profile Basic Principles

Before describing to the participants how to assess and adapt to listening-preference traits in others, the facilitator should review the following basic principles about the instrument.

*In times of stress, most people revert to their strongest listening preferences.* Because listening behaviors are habits, people usually revert to behaviors that are most familiar and comfortable when they are under stress.

*When people have little listening energy to give, they listen in ways that require the least amount of effort.* Most people would prefer to avoid difficult or challenging listening situations that require concentration when they are tired.

*Learning to adapt to others' listening preferences requires practice.* People's listening preferences are deeply entrenched. Even if they are aware that they should alter listening habits to better adapt to others, they still will need considerable practice to change behavior.

## Listening Preference Cues and Clues

There are two types of cues that participants can use to help them determine an individual's listening preference: office/environmental and personal. The following characteristics are clues that they can look for when assessing an individual's listening preference:

| | Office/Environmental Cues | Personal Cues |
|---|---|---|
| **People** | Personal pictures on walls<br>Personal objects in room or on desk<br>Some clutter on desk | Makes/Holds eye contact<br>Varies vocal inflection<br>Smiles/Nods frequently<br>May touch others during conversation |
| **Action** | Objects and furniture symmetrically arranged<br>Certificates and work-related pictures on walls<br>Clean desk<br>Desk organizers, organized bookshelves | Has brisk, firm handshake<br>Wants a neat appearance<br>Has/Wants cellular phone<br>Speaks at rapid rate<br>Shows signs of disinterest such as doodling, tapping fingers, and shifting in seat |
| **Content** | Neat stacks on desk<br>Research/Reference books near desk<br>Computer on at all times | Shows serious facial expressions<br>Uses challenging or combative vocal tones<br>Looks up frequently when processing information |
| **Time** | Has one or more clocks observable from behind desk<br>Has secretary call and remind him or her about appointments | Looks at watch often<br>Rushes visitors<br>Displays impatient facial expressions<br>Uses beepers and other signals to indicate time |

## Assessing Others

The participants can improve their accuracy if they practice assessing other people's listening preferences on a regular basis. To begin practicing, each participant should identify an individual for whom he or she would like to determine a listening preference. Using the *Listening Styles Profile,* the participant can determine whether the chosen individual is primarily people oriented, action oriented, content oriented, or time oriented. After determining the individual's preference, each participant can use this information to interact with the individual more effectively.

The participants should also consider the following strategies when communicating with others:

**People-Oriented Strategies**

- ▲ Use stories and illustrations that contain human-interest value.
- ▲ Use "we" rather than "I" in conversations.
- ▲ Use emotional examples and appeals.
- ▲ Show some vulnerability when possible.
- ▲ Use self-effacing humor or illustrations.

**Action-Oriented Strategies**

- ▲ Keep main points to three or fewer.
- ▲ Keep presentations short and concise.
- ▲ Have a step-by-step plan and label each step.
- ▲ Watch for cues of disinterest and pick up vocal pace at those points or change subjects.
- ▲ Speak at a rapid but controlled rate.

**Content-Oriented Strategies**

- ▲ Use two-sided arguments when possible.
- ▲ Provide hard data when available.
- ▲ Quote credible experts.
- ▲ Suggest logical sequences and plans.
- ▲ Use charts and graphs.

**Time-Oriented Strategies**

- ▲ Ask how much time the person has to listen.
- ▲ Try to go under time limits when possible.
- ▲ Be ready to cut out unnecessary examples and information.

- ▲ Be sensitive to nonverbal cues indicating impatience or a desire to leave.
- ▲ Get to the bottom line quickly.

**Multiple Preference Strategy**

- ▲ Examine the effects of such factors as time pressure, the communication setting, and presence of others on the individual.

## Multiple Preferences in a Group

Speakers should keep in mind that when there are three or more listeners, those listeners are likely to have multiple and/or different listening preferences. A speaker's first step should be to get a feel for the target audience by asking himself or herself the following questions:

- ▲ Who will attend the meeting?
- ▲ Will these people be attending voluntarily?
- ▲ Why are they coming and what do they hope to gain?
- ▲ Which listening preferences are these individuals most likely to have (based on their occupations and/or interests)?

When the speaker cannot answer these questions in advance, he or she may have to make an audience assessment the day of the meeting. To do this, the speaker should get to the meeting early and mingle with the audience; using the personal cues listed earlier, he or she can develop an impression about what strategy will work best. Based on the audience's reactions, the speaker can determine whether to use a more people-oriented, action-oriented, content-oriented, or time-oriented delivery style.

Although communicating might be easier if all listeners were alike, without differences people's interactions would probably be boring. Because individuals do not function as clones, participants may have difficulty identifying listener preferences correctly at first. Assessing others' listening preferences does take concentration and effort, but mastering this skill can also give speakers a competitive advantage.

The participants may make mistakes when they begin attempting to identify and adapt to other people's listening preferences. They may forget how to apply what they have learned. They may identify the wrong preference or ignore the presence of multiple preferences. At times the participants may also find that they have insufficient energy to make assessments. Even so, if they are persistent, they will discover the value of understanding their own and others' listening preferences.

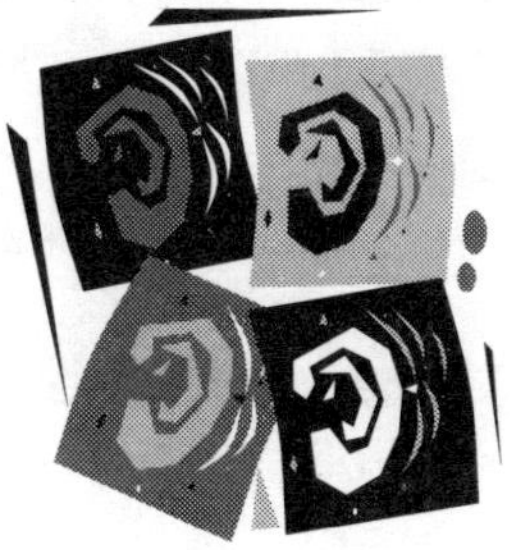

## Chapter 4
# ADMINISTRATION GUIDELINES

The *Listening Styles Profile* is designed to be administered easily and by people without experience in test administration. The facilitator should follow these procedures for the best results:

1. Distribute the instruments to the participants.
2. Make sure an answer sheet is included with each instrument.
3. Either read the directions aloud or have the participants read the instructions themselves. When explaining how to complete the instrument, encourage the participants to read along with you and to ask questions.
4. Before the participants begin, determine the listening context for them to focus on while answering the questions. For example, ask them to answer the questions based on how they listen in one of the following environments:

   - Home
   - Work
   - Overall

5. Next have the participants answer the questions on the first page of their instruments by circling the appropriate number on their answer sheets.
6. After the participants have completed the instrument, ask them to tear off the top sheets of their answer sheets. The bottom sheets provide scoring information.
7. Have the participants count the number of 4 and 5 responses they circled in the shaded areas in each section. Have them write the total number of 4 and 5 responses in each of the four section boxes. The participants should then compare their section totals. Their highest totals indicate their strongest listening preferences.
8. Ask each participant to plot his or her total score from each section box on the *Listener Preference Profile Grid.*
9. Have the participants read along while you read over the Reminders and Grid Interpretation sections from the interpretation guide.
10. Describe each preference type using the PACT acronym described in Chapter 1.
11. If time allows and the necessary materials are available, use transparencies to highlight the characteristics of each listening preference.
12. Finally, give the participants the *Listener Profile Interpretation Guide* to review.
13. Answer the participants' questions about the listening preferences using information provided in the guide.

## Key Points

In addition to completing these steps, the facilitator should emphasize the following key points for the participants:

- ▲ Listening preferences are determined by how, where, and when information is generally received; from whom it is generally received; and what types of information are generally received.
- ▲ The way people choose to receive information includes whether or not they find it easier to listen to others by telephone or face-to-face and how they prefer messages to be organized. For example, some people prefer to listen to a speaker who follows an outline, and others prefer to listen to a speaker who spontaneously includes interesting stories and examples.
- ▲ Most people's listening skills are affected by their surroundings. Some people listen best when they are in comfortable surroundings, and others listen best when they are in more formal settings.

- ▲ People have unconscious preferences, based on their energy cycles, about when it is best to receive information. Some people are morning people and others are better listeners in the afternoon or evening.
- ▲ People have likes and dislikes about the types of information they prefer listening to. Some people find technical data interesting; others find it boring.

There is no one best way to listen. As participants read about their own listening preferences, they should be encouraged not to label listener preferences as good or bad. Each preference has characteristics that can be positive or negative when taken to extremes.

## Assessing Others

The participants can use the *Listening Styles Profile* to assess others. The facilitator can use the same instructions, but he or she need only emphasize to the participants that they are evaluating someone else (for example, a spouse or coworker). The facilitator can read Chapter 3 of the guide to the participants.

# REFERENCES


Anes, E. (1987). Gender and communication. In P. Shaver & C. Hendreick (Eds.), *Sex and gender* (pp. 149-176). Newbury Park, CA: Sage.

Berryman, C. L., & Wilcox, J. R. (1980). Attitudes toward male and female speech: Experiments on the effects of sex-typical language. *Western Journal of Speech Communication, 44,* 50-59.

Boise, R., Hanley, C. P., Fansler, D., Shaughnessy, P., & Dudek, D. C. (1984). Generality of observational skill across verbal and nonverbal modes: Literature review and experimental test. *Journal of Nonverbal Behavior, 8,* 172-186.

Booth-Butterfield, M. (1984). She hears...he hears: What they hear and why. *Personnel Journal, 36,* 42.

Carli, L. L. (1989). Gender differences in interaction style and influence. *Journal of Personality and Social Psychology, 56,* 565-576.

Esposito, A. (1979). Sex differences in children's conversation. *Language and Speech, 22,* 213-220.

Hanson, R., & Mullis, R. (1985). Age and gender differences in empathy and moral reasoning among adolescents. *Child Study Journal, 15,* 181-187.

Kennedy, C. W., & Camden, C. T. (1981). Gender differences in interruption behavior: A dominance perspective. *International Journal of Women's Studies, 4,* 135-142.

Mabry, E. (1985). The effects of gender composition and task structure on small group interaction. *Small Group Behavior, 16,* 75-96.

Mahon, S. (1991). *Leadership styles and their relationship to listening styles.* Unpublished master's thesis, Auburn University, Auburn, AL.

Ray, E. B., & Bostrom, R. N. (1990). Listening in medical messages: The relationship of physician gender, patient gender, and seriousness of the illness in short- and long-term recall. In R. N. Bostrom (Ed.), *Listening behavior: Measurement and application* (pp. 128-143). New York: Guilford Press.

Seiler, W. J., Schuelke, L. D., & Lieb-Brilhart, B. (1984). *Communication for the contemporary classroom.* New York: Holt, Rinehart & Winston.

Smeltzer, L. R., & Watson, K. W. (1986). Gender differences in verbal communication during negotiations. *Communication Research Reports, 3,* 74-79.

Trotter, R. J. (1983). Baby face. *Psychology Today,* pp. 14-20.

Watson, K. W. (1984). *Listening preference profile.* New Orleans, LA: SPECTRA Communication Associates.

Watson, K. W., & Barker, L. L. (1988). *Listener preference profile.* New Orleans, LA: SPECTRA Communication Associates.

Watson, K. W., Barker, L. L., & Weaver, J. B. (March, 1992). *Development and validation of the listener preference profile.* Paper presented to the International Listening Association Convention, Seattle, WA.

Weaver, J. B., Watson, K. W., & Barker, L. L. (March, 1993). *Personality and listener preferences.* Paper presented to the International Listening Association Convention, Memphis, TN.

Wheeless, V. (1984). A test of the theory of speech accommodation using language and gender orientation. *Women's Studies in Communication, 7,* 13-22.

Zakahi, W. R., & McCroskey, J. C. (1989). Willingness to communicate: A potential confounding variable in communication research. *Communication Reports, 2,* 96-104.

Editor: Pat Gonzalez
Production Editor: Dawn Kilgore
Cover and Interior Design: Lee Ann Hubbard
Compositor: Judy Whalen

This book was edited and formatted using 486PC platforms with 8MB RAM and high resolution, dual-page monitors. The copy was produced using WordPerfect software; pages were composed with Corel Ventura software; cover and art were produced with CorelDRAW software. The text is set in eleven on fourteen Korinna and the heads are set in Neuland Bold and Futura Condensed Extra Bold. Proof copies were printed on a 400-dpi laser printer and final camera-ready output on a 1200-dpi laser imagesetter by Pfeiffer